DISPLAYS

Katherine Franco

Pilot Press
London

CONTENTS

OPENING (THE INSIDE) (THE BEGINSIDE)

Systemize my heart you
Three-person'd doll
Faced systemwide system.

Chevrolet baits
Babes. Chevrolet brakes:
And the heart
Breaks down, *too?*

Directionality
Pivots the sky
And I cry, but
Don't die.

Louis Bonacosa
Memorial
Bridge. The signs
Point toward
Signs. Systemwide!

Skydive Long
Island: but glue
Keeps my feet
On ground: as a girl

I said make it new
make it New make it
new but now all goo.

The gooey inners of
My heart abide
By the inners and signs
Of biopolytechnicaltechniques
And technologies. Beats

Like the longest drum. The droll
Drum of things thumbs
Thinginess into my system.

The system of signs thumbs
Me into being. The being
Crawls me into being.

RENUNCIATION

If desire cloisters
in fits, if it behaves

birdlike, brained, separates
you from you: you have it.

If I have you in my fist:
fits. Because it means—

—in moment, one—
moment. In slept I sleep

horrorwar. Because I did not!
Shirks me and I wisp toward:

Second night is when
it middles, grounds, pre-

dates. There is courage
in datum. Thine scourge.

THE FIRST ONE

Is sickness
so absolute
narrows so
sets so fire?
The emptiness
of horizon
is emptiness
of horizon
is emptiness.
On fire,
I set for
thee. I set
myself for thee. I
take thyself
to fire-frame and
set it. I took bone
and broke open
bank. I
wrote: in
the emptiness
of horizon. There
is a comparative politics
and I christened myself
to it. There is a
politics and I felt: in:
arms: you, things
break: I felt you.

PRACTICUM

of concrete things
of cases, waste
of tergiversation
of the fit (perfect)
of the fallible bee
of me
of how it ran
(how?)
of a frame and kind
of holding out
of – for the line
oh please don't –
don't leave me out
here

Dear Saint Theresa,

You were doctor: I doctor
Myself. I doctorly decorum.
Was there a day you chose
to reach into your core
and make it new? I feel the beating
Heart of beating pain, beating me
Alive. Is there anything else
to remind you of life-love? I ate fig
and tried. Sweetness, oh life, etc.
In reality, people are sweeter
than they seem on internet. All
feet. And mouths. And speak, opening
day up. I forgot I could stand
Up in a room and pronounce still.
Myself. I forgot the art. Shier than before,
I accept it. Like going to school first
Time, learning to speak. Okay so this
is pedagogical. I made
promise to get better.

Dear Saint Theresa,

I thought about forgiving
Myself but I couldn't now
that I could. Everything: I
Thought about everything
then hard—Collapse. I thought
about signs. There is nothing
Holy in my mouth. There is nothing.
I thought about whether
I will be desirable in spring. Desired.
I thought about the lonely dog out
on Strand 1. I thought up Strand 1
(no cloud, sea, water, lily). Waterlilies,
you call yourself precious. You didn't
choose. You called.

Dear Saint Theresa,

Now, the rat
Pain. Unglamor. So it's
the most—glamor. I fell
got myself up. I dreamt
of getting to fall
alone. So no one could see
no mind eyes sight feet
walk talk lick dick. You who
haven't known
Me alone can't know. Who
see me walk at the hours
Of day, sparkling: I don't
do that, autopilot vision
conducts the walk, but inside
Wilting, writing. Inside the invisible
Writing reaches within and tells
Me there is other world
Other word. You don't
have to dream it: latent, it
Lies. Latent it into being. Verbalize
the verb then pick
jaw off ground.

Dear Saint Theresa,

This Being called
Invisible writing calls
itself nothing because
I am not calling on it.
I am staring
at heater, heating
Me. I am staring
at me? No—
Staring. Longer days ahead were
Long because they lay
Unimagined. All the saints
on this campus give
kisses. There's no
Saints. There are people
reading about Saint Theresa
for class. There is class.
No repetition, association.
Association rims the rim.

Dear Saint Theresa,

Be the good enough
baby. The Good Enough
Mother, actually. You don't need
to parent self. You can
just be. Today, filmed
thyself. Walked through
Branches. Brechtian
branch dance. I danced
then ran. Socks
Dripping. The cold came in,
so I came on. On the trails
to the observatory trails, I saw
the light of noon. I saw the wire
dance. And myself: there I there.

Dear Saint Theresa,
[after Merrill Moore]

Same day: shower
I decided—derided
to be the good enough
Me. There's no thing
Better than being good
enough. I pat
Myself on back, girl
in mirror saw me, as I
had my big realization, naked,
we consummated
Something there. In the image
of the eye, we saw anew:
Image. It seeks a spot
to image itself whole. I like
when I use *image* as a verb
and someone I hate doesn't
know the possibility of
its verbiage. Herbs, girls,
Everything is coming
together fast. Spring
is fast. The spring time
wants you—better. And harder
to get better when you. And hard
to get better. And hard.

Dear Saint Theresa,

How can you be
in pain for years
on end without
End? I didn't Know
I strove
to seek to strove—
to dove. The doves
beckoned. No, they didn't
idiot. You don't even
know words for birds.
You wouldn't even
know a bird for a word.
You wouldn't talk
to a bird. You wouldn't
talk to anyone
about anything. Then
again, who is good enough
to hear things? Not
I. I wouldn't expect anyone
to get me at an airport,
I wouldn't expect someone
to find me worth a car.
I wouldn't expect you to pull
a Toyota out of a garage
to pull me into its backseat.

Dear Saint Theresa,

On the bench
past the bench, the one
I stood by on stand-by
waiting life to stand
up for me. It stood.
When you take
to the page, you
put down every
single foot
you know. You take everything
and splatter it. Sickening,
to do that. You do that
though. There's a literality
realer than the rain
that lives in the promise
to language that lives
in my finger, as I
put it down, as I downpat
my downy arm. There is a promise
to myself
I will honor. There is honor
and I promise
myself to it. I mean, there are
Pretenders and I am not
feigning this time. I mean
What I will say later. I maim
my name. I maimed
a name three times past,
called me new. Maim
of renewal. New. Whatness.

A SOUNDING

From the under
Am I writing

From the beating
Blunder, or night?

Just mere copy
of the copy,
I have it right,

Not right not
But not near,

Enough for
Either, or

Standing to find

The wisdom primed
O snowball prime.

This world? I, too. That much.

WITH SO EVER

Then world (day) breaks
and u cry a little (die) a little, glass
opens, reach me, glass: spit
the water back out before
I spit it: back. Spilt, split, I died a little
when you spoke to me. I shivered
a little sole, shiver, I cried a little
I leafed a little thru
the day, I broke a little bit
Thru the glass. I shifted
a little thru shifting
Sun, I sweat thru sweater
turtle neck up high, never
worn like this before, sniffed
a little, spilt milk a little, drank
little milk a little bit calcium
years to strengthen my bones
yesiree, I made peace
a little with a little piece of me
I called myself *me* a little, drifted
back into crying a bit, then saw
the strand, sought a little
piece littling myself off / on / of
the strand, sat
down on the strand, made peace
on the strand: on the strand
I made peace with the sea, me, sky
called the day open: opening
wide for the roiling rotation
rage, sea rage, me rage
pinning rage ungirding games
today saw the sea and the sea
saw me and the sea saw yesiree
the seeing sea sees me and I can breathe
because as I am a seeing breathing me
I can see and keep
clean and—time.

DENUNCIATION

Even in—world waits—
Even in—the world waited.

Becoming exception to sleep,
self-rearing, raring to enter

day, tomorrow come in
fists of horse-thyme.

In metre. To do to a tee
and follow through.

Excepting, maximized, I became
sub-human asleep. Lost

for week. Weep.
Courage: was

not-me in the face of me.
Let the order of things—

let me maintain. Let solid
ground be. Let me, sordid.

BROKERING

It did. It is good.
I met an intelligent angel.

Hey – hold up? I was there.
Pavilions and flightlessness

Were my name, but no
Matter. In morning, I scrawled

IS POETRY A FORM
OF INQUIRY in the largest

Letters like the dumbest
Bitch in the world. In

The morning, In the morning
Speech come, I

refuse rushing clear communicative
Words will come, I will

come to you My word (that
like that it stations

That it stations) Everything
I will learn everything

Precludes
Discontinuation.

STIFF OR RIGID

Look

    quick

        the heart

    LIFTS.

    Quick   Quick

    LOOK.

    LOOK!

    Looking

        at you,

      my heart
      looked
      a bit
      off
      + fried

PROBLEM PLAY

Why is human behavior

Not an eye? Every day

I stunt to write my ethics.

Not waiting I wait

Kindness to yield for presence. I yield.

I have never felt anger I have never felt
The crisp rage at total end. A leg's

Abstention. Obstinate. Anger is

The unmanageable surface. Cressida. I have

Been described as contractual
But I have never laid down terms

For anything

I am quick

For anything

OUTSIDE TACTICS

Today is akin It is
mined and skinned.

Briny edge. I know
Now that was joy.

It was pure stuck.
How? I licked

My lip. The groundlings
Sung. The firmament

sung. The feet of footed
footed sounds too
Sung. Wrung down,

But it was not a dream. What
Calls from memory is not

Not not a dream. That flesh
And skin. The firmest

Firmament could not.

When all lilted
attractive. I was briny-
edged, But it was me. By

The river that was
Me. I was the sibilant

I had always
inside And it was me.

LITTLE SYMBOLS

I.

SO HERE ARE THINGS TO THINK ON
THAT OUGHT TO MAKE ME BRAVE

I
missed
this ground.

I
was not
foundered

I
left it said

Even Aristotle
Was unmanned
And I drew

For flight

II.

It is devotion.
Yes to

How the firmament
Sung. Instead,

Professing
Confessing
To

The firmament was new
Then to

Who was looking

The light screened
Thin. Win.

I felt we
Winners, win.

Gravelledground
thringing bringing
Through the rush

Like a twined souled
Angel. If you were

To walk toward
me, I would

shirk

Shirked
And

III.

Little-stoned
Primed clerical
To a cone or

Many gemmed
Gold will muster

You will return

You will come back

You came back

I did not could have not known

That these own rubies

Would efface. My kind

It scares

To know

IV.

Raggedly, traggedly
She walked.

Still gold
And mine. The stakes,
Haunts.

Come to my haunts
To knight. Relatively
Made Relativity Easy.

And and and and
when she came to the pause
Everyone stopped in track.

They saw the sentinel and pressured
Down. I saw it. I was there.

Everyone misdirected, then flew.
But you: not you.

They all made it out except you.

V.

Then the septillion
Reptilian sceptre
Flew. We who grew
Knew. Encased
In reeves, I took it.

We who came
Began to name
Wherein how
We should not
Have been saved.

EXTANT

Not one
Synonym for
Striation

Not, or
near, Body. In
the morning

in the morning
they were each
other's face—I was
not in that morning.

ROGUE AT JUNE'S END

My eyes are liquid flesh.
Since, we could not have it.
Look into the eye and tell: I am not more
Than liquid nor flesh but the hybridized
Mechanism possessing mechanics
To call itself, if not grow, Anew.
Not 'to be', not to make an 'ontologically'
Savvy sign, nor to make friends
With the rotten every, but to be
A crude reactant to daily life. Reticence.
On the street, on every street, one person
Is bound to cease at a point. They miss
the ground. Even if not the imaginary anything
Could. *Here* we called it. Flesh, this pulsing
Surface – I know it is a surface, it is new and always
Changing, unthinking, it never tells
More or gives nouns – this surface grants
None other than one perfectible sign.

TEN POINTS

Why is narrative
a socially
symbolic act?

Well

Yeah, I have a daughter.
Yeah, I am autonomous. I know

Cybernetics. My daughter feels good
That I feel. Post

Studies is here. Jargon
Is here. I feel that

I feel. If I have
To say *you*, you

are not

Here. But and and and

The third bridge
and divers near and

the force of the coldest
After

(Striations) (mine)

Asked the
All Knowing

All, I asked, it

Answered
you

Will
Know to

DISPLAYS

If screens are toxicological and time
is general: where does that leave

the mix of things? A generalized road it

hits me, I think
it means attachment
reigns (no subj. or comment) it

means (outside
thinking how) when

Outside, sans toxins,
sans sans, comic
sans sans, comic
medium, *medius*: why
be w/ (twice) me if time
is generalizable? False

Flatterers. The generalizable is
shame. That shame
was general. Screen-
emitted, compounded, this
fate, bagged, usable.

AIM-INHIBITED KISSING

Morning!   Reading
On a bench—ran   into
one (then)

                    Another

Saw   Another

So lovely   To see

Another

(I CAN'T THINK SERIOUS
SERIOUS WHEN I WANT)

                (X)

(I HAVE TO ACT)

(WHAT WILL X
SAY TO Y TO   ANOTHER?)

(I WILL SAY)

                (Y)

(I WILL SAY I WILL)

(THE OTHER NIGHT)

(THE OTHER SAY)

(THE OTHERS SAY)

On the bench, I sit
and pare thine own
nails, wracking
tackylittlerhymes
rack of lamb, blood
No just a bit of speak
for one good lucky
person who gets to hear
A bit today to hear do
You want to be the one
to hear a bit to hear
The bit to hear

EXERCISING THE SPIRIT

I.

Let's understand 'les vignerons.'
Googling, ogling, I think, I don't
understand anything I say and no one believes me.

Let's put on a robe. Let's put a robe on you.

I was in the country. Out back when you called.

Opening the shower
After showering to forgo mold:
For my sister.

Misery is trag. *Tragacanth*. Tragakantha. A wretched
Thing forlorn. Lichens: no: over-

Grown.
Screeching, children: they don't say
(*You don't say!*). My family

Is a family. To declare everything
Is a task and fair. To make oneself again. Melancholy crop.

II.

To die by your sword would be trag.
I walked the maze a day
someone shipped in

bonbons.
That's not trag. Sweetest thing

In the world and I can feel it slow
Enough. Walking the maze vowed to walk.

Chewing gum
I vowed to chew. Vow to bear a stanza
That bores. Like, that gives birth
To the history

Of ideas, ideation, machination, machine-like

likeness machine. Right, can do
no wrong. Except.

III.

When people do no wrong except
wrongs, oh I didn't think you could
laugh. Putting forth

A statement seems like putting
forth a claim, but actually
It means to be

Checked. Like,
by sword.

(speech-sword hacked daemon-like fresh)
Need to be hacked with a sword.

Laughter is endorsement. Sponsoring
A speech act is a hack. Even
if boring Even

IV.

If I know words and images ignite the human
Soul and I know life is a condition

of liveliness and an inner
Life and I know I have an inner

Life and know: we ate, sea sawing

Have you been to Berlin? Spent your time
In an underground motion filled (I don't care

About Berlin—I just like speaking of any

Thing because it means
we can stay in speech
in) ground: when you called
me, called me

back to ground, I was just
Bugged, stomached, clipped.

RANGE

Being all East Coast
But yeah the sea

Is it left to me is

the grandeur (why the sea
Why the sea yeah. Yeah.)

The sea. Running

Toward my life bit my

Cheek. Running toward

My life my life my life

Running toward (not yet
Dead dead is dead)

Eternity laden Creature not

Left me razed bearing
My teeth at the sun

November then. Liveness.

THE SENSE OF SENSE OF SENSE OF SENSE OF SENSE OF SENSE

Not one synonym for *striation*. Still wonder
whether people mean this, when they say
Writing. Realism: I love you. Seances and sounds
of kids: I love you. In visions I still myself to one
gesture of throwing myself to the tide. Picturing. 1
do not need to publish everything. (Do NOT
'publish everything'.) Keenly. Deny people +
yourself some things. Need to keep some of it
(words) 4 ourselves. Life, air, things are moving at
very fast fastidious paces + things — they changed,
ok? You said. Rods, tides, foes, sense, sense,
senses. No, I know, I'm speaking, to me, too, but
you're, I can't do much for you right now. Yeah,
Sure, I am veined lest running. Else————

4 DECEMBER

Tree so finely drawn
outside window I drew
my blinds. Cruel elected: and you

say things (life—life) lie
close, so
hard, things
lie, I was so

close, could
slit throats if falling

into standing-by

one girl on one street, crying over
river, partner, her partner looking
scary domestic—domestic, it scares
I did nothing (*drowning, he was*)

Paralysis: palatial. I was close
to her and I chose

the rail, she was
running, I was running
the engine-body handed down
to me for me, this thing I was
saving to salvage.

CRITIQUES

Suitors ask me
why I write.
I hate them. Love
Need not require
explication nor explanation.

Listening to
music I
commit to
the first secs,
Commit. Noncommital

less. I don't
Hate them. I
hate the way
they want me
To answer. On

The freeway, I am
just me. I am just
typing me. Who
turns that down? I
Feel me. I feel

Suitors did not spit
I'm my eye, in

My eye, but it sure
Feels like the maelstrom
Of my life come to
Rage or with the land

The sword reified my heart
Do you know what I mean?

Suitors didn't spit. Do you know
What I mean, Being
let me be. I watch,
Watch the ocean bend
Drive the coast line
Ventura, or.

MEASURE + DISCPLINE

and I am
meeting you
soon + light +
still remember
you, it
was fun, I
remember, break,
break, fun
fun riverriverrunrun,
and I wonder if
this will be my last
of the year
+ thank god +
thank god
mother father, even
if + thank
thank you
thank you
+ I think I am
healthier +
+ braver +
I touched the code,
even for a sec +
made sound run
+ run

FASHION

One likes one
Personed, Hesitant
Incarnate. Like I like
my friends to win
Institutions. She
best. West. Where
Here. Where
With All. Line,
Run thick. Please
Don't leave me. Bit, in
mid-April, we
relocated from horses.
The horses came.
The groundlings and
the pinkmoon, too
Mere. Benefits
for uptake. Go
point to the point
where the awful
brilliant thing felled.
Came. Coming.
Numbing. It fell
In parts. That is that
but in form.

LAMENTATION

Godhead. I keep seeing foxes.
I will continue

ruining—this lamentation.
I will ruin my life by virtue

of naming my self
to this life. Crystals. Droll.

When I imagine lamentation,
I imagine laminating

Sheets. Still
gold and mine. Thine

heart: collect thee from thine
Heart and be free.

But know I
could never be, I could—

Things and Forms:
I see you. I was looking

Towards stringent enclavement.
Facsimile is likeness. Which means.

LIKE: LIKE

Indulgence. Little
mouse, rats,
everything will
happen again.
Likeness is like
flying. Fits
perfect. Weil
happens in
the while.
Mean-time.
Lying. Not
meant
to do
anything
– to say
You – if
'expanded
explanation tends
to spoil
the lion's leap'?
We leapt together.
The river crowned.
I spoil everything
but language
leaps, too.

PURE, OR RESTLESS

For JA (b. 1999)

Agency: here. Action:

Phrases   here. I don't know

          (*to see the inside of my mind*)

Walking,   another practice

Then knowledge   -formation. I go

To the road

as a practice.

              I go to this road

              To find my friend

              On the other side.

MOULDING

We laugh for death because
The eye does not speak.

If the river
goes to
a point
visible to
no human
eye, might

I hold up
My frogged-dignity
and aspect-like
Stupor today? Crisp.

Or, just dogged. If
not day?
If wrong
To listen to

– well, drawing, but
Also. Death-gone
sprawl. Antagonistic
Lilt-like. Garnet-driven.

THE LAST DAYS OF DISCO

To speak of the hill

is   disservice:

To speak to another

is to   service:

To explicate systems

        At the top of the hill

                one knows
                an upward
                    way,

                forgetting viscid
                ground, or mud, is

                imprecise to
                normal life.

Righting oneself
one seeks a hill. Righting
wrongs, one repays
everyone. In one system
of belief seeking repagination
on grounds. There is nothing above

the hill. At the hill, some twosome speaks

in vernacular. To hear it

           is a disservice if

one is not in motion.

              But feet dig, in

    speech lifts.

                    Returning to the world, mere
motions, a bird speaks in vernacular. Hear

vernacular   disservices   language   disservices

the ground. But without air,
                              without

light, without   speaking of a without and in turn

loving the other, without

                  staunch belief
in sprites, without conditions

for other life
one   needs   everything.

CONSERVATION TRACK

I paused
for every
turnstile

I held
up every

critique to
the world

to the light
of day, or

maybe I
was just
cold. If

you love
your life

what is
there

to be
said

for what
is said?

I am
taking
it, you
know,

to the place, ferns
freezed out, but
not waiting

ACKNOWLEDGEMENTS

I write and publish in memory of Jamie Albrecht, 1999-2023.

I am grateful to the editors of the journals and anthologies in which some of these poems first appeared: *DATABLEED*, *Juked*, *Ludd Gang*, *The Oxonian Review*, Pilot Press, *Prelude*, and *Yalobusha Review*.

"Like: Like" features text by Kathy Acker and Marianne Moore. "Little Symbols" features text by A.E. Housman.

I am fortunate to have landed in the orbit of my publisher and editor, Richard Porter. Pilot Press has made the practice of publication lively and generative in ways I never quite imagined. Rich, thank you for your commitment to my work.

I have waited for this opportunity to thank my teachers: Lotus Do, Simone Dubrovic, Noah Falck, Adam Guy, Christopher Hood, Deborah Laycock, Min Jin Lee, Stephen Mak, Ricardo Maldonado, Maya C. Popa, Misha Rai, Grace Schulman, Orchid Tierney, Dirk Van Hulle, Monique Vogelsang, Keith S. Wilson, and others.

In many ways, I came back to poetry at State of the Arts (SOTA) at the University of Oxford in 2019. Thank you to the organisers and friends who supported my work and listened to me read. My thanks to the *Kenyon Review*, especially my inspiring students at the KR Young Writers Workshop 2021.

Zoe, for reading my poems for the last decade. This friendship has been a foundation. You know. All the rest of my friends, of course, and my parents.

I turn to my sister Lauren Franco at every turn. I do so now in tremors of gratitude.

Katherine Franco is a writer and artist. Her work appears in *Prelude*, *Jacket2*, and *Juked*, among others. She is a PhD student in English at the University of California, Berkeley.

Published in the U.K. by Pilot Press
Copyright © Katherine Franco 2023
ISBN 978-1-7393649-3-9
All rights reserved
Printed on 100% recycled paper